from
THE RELUCTANT MESSENGER

IN THE
BEGINNING

Candice M. Sanderson

CLARK
PRESS

An Imprint of Crystalline Wisdom Path, LLC
Naples, Florida

Copyright © 2022 by Candice M. Sanderson

All rights reserved. No part of this publication may be reproduced, distributed, or transmitted in any form or by any means, including photocopying, recording, or other electronic or mechanical methods, without the prior written permission of the publisher, except in the case of brief quotations embodied in critical reviews and certain other noncommercial uses permitted by copyright law. For permission requests, contact the author through www.CandiceSanderson.com.

Parties interested in quantity sales or autographed copies may contact Clark Press through the author's webpage at www.CandiceSanderson.com.

CLARK
PRESS

Published by Clark Press, Naples, Florida
Clark Press is an imprint of Crystalline Wisdom Path, LLC

Cover, interior design, and formatting by MaryDes Designs

From the Reluctant Messenger: In the Beginning
By Candice M. Sanderson
First Edition
10 9 8 7 6 5 4 3

This book is based on material from *The Reluctant Messenger*
Library of Congress Control Number: 2017918547

ISBN 979-8-9858228-3-0 (Paperback)
ISBN 979-8-9858228-4-7 (Hardback)

To Phillip, Cassie, Lorelai, Shalane,

and Daryl

"In the beginning God created the heaven and the earth."

— Genesis 1:1, King James Version

CONTENTS

Preface..13

Introduction...17

In the Beginning..21

The Word...33

Acknowledgements..61

from
THE RELUCTANT MESSENGER

IN THE
BEGINNING

PREFACE

In August of 2013, my life as a pragmatic psychologist abruptly ended when I began receiving messages from other-worldly sources. I relied on my clinical training to help me through these remarkable times.

My courses to become a psychologist taught me how to be an objective observer. I automatically slipped into this role, recording my extraordinary experiences in real time. Shortly afterwards, I would sit at my computer and painstakingly transcribe my narratives. Within months, I had amassed hundreds of pages detailing my encounters.

Preface

The next step was also second nature: investigate my findings. When after-the-fact research verified much of the data I had collected, I began to understand my experiences were more than just fascinating events.

Each search engine hit chiseled at the foundations of my belief system until one day I could no longer deny what I had unearthed: I had stumbled into new realms of existence. My research offered authentic proof—if there is such a thing—that reality is more than what the physical senses measure.

Suspending my understanding of life made room for new truths to arrive. I learned to embrace Nikola Tesla's philosophy that the secrets of the universe lie within energy, vibrations, and frequencies.

Not only have I used them to explore the outer edges of human consciousness, but these once-kept mysteries have reshaped my understanding of life. They have become the prisms through which I have come to know myself and the world around me.

This series, *From the Reluctant Messenger*, is an opportunity to reexamine a few accounts from my earlier books while offering a venue for my new ventures—some of which have expanded the boundaries of my beliefs more than I thought possible.

From the Reluctant Messenger offers bite-sized, unique glimpses into non-ordinary realms of existence. As we slip into these often-unmarked territories of spirit, we just might hear the whisperings of truth that hide below the surface of awareness. Perhaps we'll see how our destinies unfold in the subtle play and patterns of synchronicity in what we thought were our ordinary lives.

I invite you to stretch your imagination and join me as we travel beyond the limits that have held us in the past. Take a deep breath, and let's take the plunge into some of these adventures that led this ordinary person on an extraordinary journey into the unknown.

Welcome aboard!

Candice M. Sanderson
www.CandiceSanderson.com
Naples, Florida

INTRODUCTION

There are specific moments that define each one of us. We may not know it at the time; we might learn it later. But for some of us, it's obvious. You can put your finger on it, that definable indelible moment when everything changes.

My story began on a dull gray Wednesday in August 2013. As I exited the garage for a short commute to work, nothing in the predawn sky suggested my life was about to change. Little did I know that strange and mysterious events would soon become part of my everyday existence.

Introduction

As a psychologist, I lived a logical, predictable life; I only trusted what I could measure with my physical senses. Anything beyond those parameters couldn't be real. I identified them as anomalies ranging from wishful thinking to fantasy to psychosis.

Imagine my astonishment when I became immersed in a sea of unspeakable beauty, floating in a realm that existed beyond the world of physicality. Within a profound glittering silence, words of wisdom drifted into my awareness, allowing me to peek into unknown dimensions.

Message by message, my ordinary life changed. And as new landscapes unfolded, I began researching these messages from this great beyond, seeking answers to questions I had never pondered.

Each search engine hit changed me, lifting a curtain that allowed further access to a universe others could not see. The farther I threw my anchor beyond the physical, the deeper I landed in the intangible realms that some call spirit.

Several people have described me as psychic. Am I? Maybe. But being psychic isn't reserved for the world of the occult or in darkened rooms for séances. It's a skill anyone can learn.

We can fine-tune the brain to register subtle cues surrounding us. We constantly gather information, but most don't recognize it in real time.

Once I began navigating the world through the lens of energy, I realized that vibrations and frequencies propel us through interdimensional channels. This is how we access these strange new worlds that somehow feel familiar.

I now understand we exist in more than one dimensional space and that these extraordinary realms of consciousness are merely different aspects of a singular truth.

Throughout these often-astonishing travels into the unknown, never has my voyage been as profound as this episode I'm about to share.

Your invitation awaits. Grab my hand as we slip through a tiny tear in the fabric of consciousness and travel back to where everything began—creation. Welcome to *In the Beginning*.

IN THE BEGINNING

How could I explain the unexplainable? How could I share this story with others when I had trouble believing it myself? My experiences confused me, yet they filled me with awe.

It had been two years since my world opened to the realms of the nonphysical. Just as I felt comfortable interacting with star systems, angels, and ascended masters, an even more astonishing event began.

Although my non-ordinary encounters had vastly expanded my worldview, they paled in comparison to what began on September 29, 2015. In the wee hours of that momentous day, the life I had known changed. The incidents confused me, and all I could do was watch as these inexplicable events unfolded against the backdrop of my daily life.

I struggled to process and understand the meaning of these experiences. Each day, another piece of the puzzle floated into my awareness, but on the fifth day, I had an epiphany. I breathed a sigh of relief as the remaining parts fell into place, completing the mosaic.

The backdrop to the event was an enormous influx of energy that had invaded my body a few weeks earlier; I had become a whirlwind of activity. This took me by surprise.

This adrenaline rush pushed my bedtime three or four hours later than usual, and my customary nine to ten hours of sleep vanished. Instead, I rarely dozed more than three hours each night.

As a psychologist, I am aware of the effects of sleep deprivation: memory loss, irritability, fatigue, impaired thinking. Yet none of these happened. I went to work and functioned well, in fact, better than usual. I was alert as I moved through my days with surprising clarity. I felt vibrant.

My professional training recognized this contradiction as a paradoxical effect, yet nothing could explain why it occurred. How could a significant reduction in sleep enhance my work ability? It didn't make sense.

My online search to understand this phenomenon was futile, leaving me with more questions than answers.

I knew *why* I couldn't sleep—the extraordinary energy that had invaded my life—but the reasons behind it remained a mystery. What had brought this influx of energy? What caused it?

After another sleepless night in mid-September, I got out of bed a couple of hours past midnight. An urge swept through every fiber of my body. I didn't understand it, but I knew I must obey this powerful impulse that commanded me to run.

Driven by the same inexplicable force that had interrupted my sleep the past several weeks, I put on shoes and shorts and went outside.

Although I had been a runner in high school, that ended with my first serious back injury in 1986. Months afterward, I still required help to get out of bed, and I could not walk unassisted. After multiple spinal surgeries, my back and neck contained enough hardware to set off security machines at airports, so my decision to run shocked me.

But run, I did. I jogged almost a mile on that first day, and by midweek, I had tripled my distance to three miles. This felt incredible, unbelievable.

What made me race through my neighborhood like someone half my age? I hadn't a clue, but something was stirring. As my thoughts drifted toward the messengers, I intuitively knew there was a connection. This unexplained rush of energy must be preparing me for something with them. I would soon find out.

For another two weeks, I slipped into a pattern of going to bed late and then waking a couple of hours past midnight. I would get up, dress, and go outside to run. Sleep didn't seem to matter anymore.

Although I had adjusted to my new life as a resurrected runner, and I could breeze through my days with ease, nothing could have prepared me for what was about to happen.

While running at 3:00 a.m. on September 29, 2015, a detailed event played in my mind's eye with such intensity that it consumed me. I stopped dead in my tracks.

With my physical body motionless, a tumultuous whirlwind of energy propelled my awareness, my consciousness, into a deep, cosmic abyss.

Darkness surrounded me, yet almost imperceptible movements captured my attention. These delicate black shadows drifted like transparent chiffon scarves caught in a slow-moving night breeze. I was mesmerized.

The pattern became more defined, and the swirling vapors coalesced into a whirling haze that spiraled around the perimeter of the abyss. Without warning, the incoming clouds became frenetic and collapsed inward toward a central point where a small glimmer of light had begun to glow.

As these roiling waves rushed toward this mysterious spark in the center of the void, I braced for a head-on collision.

The anticipated crash did not materialize. Instead, these energy surges reversed direction and arced backward, creating a three-dimensional torus that encircled the light. The torus swirled in its signature donut-shaped configuration, becoming more powerful with each second.

In the Beginning

As the toroidal field intensified, so did the light within its center. I watched it strengthen, becoming a dazzling, magnificent radiance that was brighter than a thousand suns. Yet as quickly as the wave of energy had begun, the frenzied movement halted.

Time stopped, yet I was still there, existing in the silent, measured pauses between thoughts, in the absolute stillness of this suspended world, this new dimension evolving in front of my eyes.

Then I saw an ever-so-slight movement in the light, followed by another and another until the light began to pulse like a giant heart. A new life had been born.

A blanket of divine serenity and peace covered me, yet on some mystifying level, I intuitively knew I was in the center of the calm before a storm. In anticipation of whatever might come, I held my breath.

Suddenly, my awareness hurtled from the abyss, and the activity below faded. From my new vantage point, the faraway, dream-like scene captivated me. Within seconds, I understood why my position had changed.

From far above the chaos, the brilliant light slowly detonated, and billions of photons shot across the horizon as far as I could see. I gasped. The intensity and enormity of the event sent shockwaves through my body, almost overpowering me. Yet the unwavering splendor and magnificence of the eruption also filled me with wonder.

I wept. I had just witnessed creation.

Although the initial experience lasted less than two minutes, these incredible scenes repeated over the next five days. During my early morning runs, an extended version replayed in my mind's eye.

These uncut adaptations offered closer looks as parts of the vision slowed, allowing new details to bloom into existence.

Each day, messages swarmed my awareness, suggesting different interpretations of the images bombarding my mind's eye. On day five, it ended. This collection of multidimensional perspectives of the director's cut of creation was complete.

I learned of matters that had been foreign to me: black holes, singularities, gravity wells, waveforms, cosmic voids, dark energy, expansion and contraction of the universe, sacred geometry, stargates, wormholes, event horizons, entrainment, photon belts, and how stars form.

IN THE BEGINNING

My understanding of creation expanded astronomically. For reasons I cannot begin to fathom, I saw views of creation as it related to religion, energy, physics, quantum mechanics, cosmology, and astronomy.

I tried to make sense of these bizarre experiences but couldn't. As I went about my daily life, questions constantly simmered in the background, begging for answers. Finally, explanations arrived early Sunday morning on October 4, 2015.

I returned from my early morning run around 3:30 a.m. and showered. It would be several hours before the sun would rise. As I sipped my morning coffee, I thought about these past five days; these were the most significant experiences I'd ever had.

My brain was spinning with the same questions I'd had for weeks: Why had the vision repeated each day? Why had the messengers shown me different views of the same event? But this time, an answer followed my barrage of thoughts: I had become an "instrument of the word."

When I heard this phrase, the first line of the prayer of St. Francis of Assisi crossed my mind,

"Lord, make me an instrument of your peace."

As an instrument of the word, I realized I had been named an agent, a representative. I was to be a translator for this new energy that powered my unexpected stint as a runner and the vision of creation.

A new understanding emerged, and I realized why I had seen different versions. Each perspective appeals to a specific group of people.

Although each consortium used a different vocabulary, they describe the same thing—creation. With creation at the center of the hub, the individual views were no longer separate. Like spokes of a wheel, these interpretations became a diverse yet collective perspective supporting a singular truth.

I exhaled deeply, releasing a huge sigh of relief. This new information provided answers, but my reprieve was short-lived. The turmoil of the past few weeks returned as I realized that this revelation generated more questions.

Doubt raised its ugly head. How could this message be true? Me, an instrument of the word?

I had been channeling for a couple of years, and my research verified many communications I had received. But this was different.

Could it be wishful thinking? Although I've never thought of myself as being motivated by ego, perhaps I was. Not only was it difficult to trust this explanation but it was also impossible to verify.

The weight of my experiences and these thoughts descended on me, plunging me into depths of despair. My eyes filled with tears as I tried to catch my breath. I needed help. One word flashed through my mind, a word that surprised me: church.

It had been years since I'd sat in a sanctuary and listened to a sermon, so where would I go? A smile crossed my face when I thought of Unity Church of Naples. I had recently attended an evening meditation there, and the kind people at the event welcomed me with open arms.

Yes, I would seek refuge at this sacred church. I knew this divine place of spiritual worship would offer an escape from the drama and excitement of the past few weeks.

When it was time to leave home, I added the location to the GPS on my phone and headed to the garage. Within half an hour, I arrived.

I pulled into the remote winding drive that meanders through a beautifully wooded parking lot. I found an empty spot, and as I stepped outside my car, I took a deep breath. I was already feeling more peaceful than I had in weeks.

I smiled and nodded toward a few groups of friendly, familiar-looking people as I made my way toward the sanctuary's opened doors.

I thanked the kind volunteer who handed me the Sunday bulletin with information about today's program. I slipped into a seat near the back of the sanctuary and made myself comfortable.

The enormity of the past five days descended on me without warning, and I brought my hands to my face to hide an unexpected wave of grief and confusion. Minutes passed before I could open my eyes to survey my surroundings.

Still struggling to contain my composure, I glanced down as tears spilled on the opened pamphlet resting in my lap. As the words from the bulletin came into focus, my heart began to pound.

I gasped when I realized this house of worship offered more than shelter from my personal storm. It provided what I thought was impossible: verification. I knew this uncanny confirmation could only have come from one source—the messengers.

I held the key in my hands, the proof, the validation. At the top of the Sunday bulletin was "October 4" and in large letters, "The Feast of St. Francis of Assisi."

The Feast of St. Francis? A sudden understanding, larger than words, swept through my body as I studied the bulletin. I held my breath at this aha moment.

The St. Francis connection illuminated the words from the messengers, confirming the reasons behind the multidimensional interpretations of the vision: I had become an instrument.

I exhaled, sending waves of peace and serenity throughout my body. I thanked the messengers for clarification and validation of the most significant event of my life. I smiled, and without warning, I whispered these words: "I see the Light."

THE WORD

The message begins with a striking similarity to Genesis 1:1-2 of the King James Version of the Bible, "In the beginning God created the heaven and the earth. And the earth was without form, and void; and darkness was upon the face of the deep. And the Spirit of God moved upon the face of the waters."

In the beginning God [religious personification] *looked about and saw nothingness, for there was nothing and is nothing except Him. There was no form. There was no space. There were no boundaries* [cosmic void]. *He is. He is all that is. There is nothing more.*

As He is everything and everywhere, there is nothing, no thing where He is not [describing the Holy Spirit of God]. *Yet there was a desire for expression, the expression of His Oneness.*

Notice how Genesis' key words "without form," "void," and "darkness" describe the messengers' cosmic void: "no form," "no space," and "no boundaries."

The message continues:

Within the dark void, He called forth the formless energies of all that is to come to Him. He did this with a great exhalation of breath [expansion of the universe caused by dark energy]. *His breath continued to the far reaches, awakening His life force, and throughout everywhere, the energy obeyed the summons. And so it began.*

This enormous exhalation within the void engages dark energy, a mysterious and invisible force that composes up to 72% of everything in the universe (Astronomy.swin.edu.au).

Astronomers speculate dark energy repulses

everything within its reach. This negative pressure is the opposite of gravity; it repels objects.

In the next paragraph, we see the Creator inhale, thus completing the life-affirming cycle of breathing, i.e., exhaling and inhaling.

He then inhaled, using His breath to pull those energies toward Him. This inhalation created a vacuum [cosmic void]. *With the reversal of His breath, the energy contracted* [contraction of the universe]; *it became a magnet* [gravity] *for those formless energies, pulling them to His center.*

Comparing the expansion and contraction of the universe to the Creator's massive inhalation and exhalation piques my interest. My research reveals surprising results. I discover the Big Bounce, a lesser-known cosmological model for the origin of the universe.

According to ScienceAlert.com, the universe operates like a balloon, bouncing between extreme states of contraction and expansion. My eyes crinkle into a smile when I realize how this theory eerily resembles the inhalation/exhalation process described by the messengers.

Proponents of the Big Bounce suggest this

model offers a fuller explanation for our humble beginnings than the better-known Big Bang theory. They assert the latter model isn't necessarily incorrect, but it's incomplete, accounting for only the expansion phase of our origins.

> *Those energies swirled in all directions, gathered together, turned, and raced toward the Source of the call. And from all directions, those energies came.*
>
> *Megalithic waves came forth like a gigantic tsunami, gathering strength and force as they raced toward the Source of the calling. As the waves approached the Light in the center of the vortex created by His summons, they crashed into each other.*
>
> *Waves of dark energy collapsed into particles* [formless to form/waves to particles: quantum physics]. *The energy began to enfold upon itself, creating layers upon layers* [building a torus field], *flooding into that deep center of stillness, the vacuum that had called them home.*

Quantum physics, a sublevel of reality, explains how a wave can instantaneously become a particle. QuantumPhysicsLady.org reports this seemingly impossible conversion occurs the moment someone detects it. This interaction with intelligent energy, i.e., the observer, precipitates the waves-to-particles transformation.

Sciencedaily.com corroborates that finding. They report the mere act of observation modifies objects on a quantum level, allowing waves to behave like particles.

The observer effect ties religion to science. The "Light" in the center of the vortex is the Creator wishing for self-expression. This observer is the intelligence that initiates changes in the quantum field.

The outer waves of energy continued to contract and rush toward His center. The great toroidal field of energy relentlessly circled then collapsed, repeating the pattern of building and collapsing, over and over. This great vortex, this boundless vacuum, gathered more and more photons of all that is until it formed the first black hole.

Supporting documentation from National Aeronautics and Space Administration's website verifies several aspects of the message. The vortex (cosmic void), labeled as a "boundless vacuum" by the messengers, aligns with NASA's description of the formation of black holes.

The repeating pattern of building and collapsing mimics the Creator's immense inhalation and exhalation mentioned in earlier passages. We see a religious personification when the messengers describe the waves of energy contracting toward "His" center.

The messengers' comparison of the process to the Creator reveals its significance; this is a report of the *first* black hole—creation has begun.

The crashing of these energies into the center of the Creator produced awareness. Rising awareness observed as form grew from the formless; boundaries developed, creating space where no space had existed before there were boundaries. Awareness created consciousness.

I had to return to the beginning of the message to better understand the connection to religion. The opening paragraph describes how the "nothingness" of the void (the formlessness of the Holy Spirit) has a "desire for expression, the expression of His Oneness."

We now see the formless (Holy Spirit) manifest

as form (the Father) as a direct result of the Holy Spirit's yearning for self-expression.

As the torus continued to build and recycle energy, its center became more powerful as awareness and consciousness intermingled and increased astronomically. Yet stillness, centeredness, and holiness filled with power and love resided deep within the center.

This ever-building field of dynamic energy created energy fusion, a nuclear reaction of these mighty energies.

Corroborating this information requires research. I pull out my laptop and start investigating this topic that is so foreign to me. When I land on LumenLearning.com, I discover hydrogen and helium atoms are the primary components of stars.

Their dense concentration causes a nuclear fusion reaction in the star's core, confirming the words from the messengers.

As two hydrogen atoms bond into a single helium atom to create nuclear fusion, the ensuing force thrusts outward against the inward pull of gravity. When the energy reaches the star's outer surface, it sends electromagnetic radiation into space, thus creating the star's bright glow.

I continue reading the website with great interest. I smile at my next discovery: The same nuclear fusion occurring within stars also happened during creation. Lumen Learning theorizes the nuclei of two hydrogen atoms fused into one helium atom during the birth of the universe.

When I examine Energy.gov/science's website, more evidence emerges. Not only did this new search substantiate the specific nuclear reaction during creation, but they conclude their report with a remarkable statement: "Since then (referring to creation), the nuclear reactions in the life and death of stars have formed most of the other nuclei in the universe."

It is, indeed, the beginning.

This nuclear reaction, this massive shift of energy, produced Light, brilliant and powerful beyond measure [hydrogen-to-helium fusion creating a star's light: LumenLearning.com].

These great energies created a single point of Light, an energy called the singularity.

A star was born.

I find several sources that connect the singularity to creation. The Big Bang theory (Space.com) suggests that 13.7 billion years ago, our universe emerged from a singularity.

Bruce E. Morton, Ph.D. from the University of Hawaii School of Medicine, has an article that captures my attention. Its title, "Galactic Singularity Engine: Origin of Life," confirms the role of a singularity in creation (Hawaii.edu).

This singularity, this brilliant star, exemplified the awareness of God, the Creator, expressing. It represented the life force of our God, consciousness, creating the great central sun/star.

This great Light began to beat like a giant heart, taking on a life of its own. Its vibrations matched the music of all that is.

As I receive the message, a vivid vision flashes into my awareness. As far as my eyes could see are millions of diamonds scattered on top of black cloth-type material. Seconds later, I notice movement below the structure, as if an invisible hand pinches and tugs the cloth downward.

An avalanche of diamonds hurtles toward the gravitational abyss, spilling over the rim like water down a drain. In one fell swoop, the gems plummet through the chasm, landing at the bottom of the gravitational well.

As the diamonds cluster, I can no longer see their individual forms; they dissolve into a brilliant point of light.

Much later, I research singularities on NASA's website, and I find supporting evidence. NASA reports a black hole is an area in the cosmos where the gravitational pull is so strong that light cannot escape.

This cosmic phenomenon occurs when matter from an exploding star compresses into a tiny area, creating a singularity in the center of the black hole. The singularity, "a point of infinite density and gravity," is so strong that it forms a space-time boundary called an event horizon.

NASA's information mirrors the vision: The diamonds on the black cloth represent stars against a black sky. The gravitational pull beneath the dark material creates a black hole. The compressed diamonds (stars) form a singularity.

Although I don't comprehend it in real time, NASA's research pulls back a curtain on what the messengers show me. I am amazed at the accuracy of the vision, and I finally understand what I saw:

a singularity forming within a black hole.

His energy continued, creating more awareness and consciousness, strengthening the singularity, that great central sun/star, even more. He looked at what He had done, and this pleased Him. He smiled and said, "This is good."

Note the uncanny similarity of the message to Genesis 1:31 (KJV), "And God saw everything that he had made, and behold, it was very good." Once again, the messengers anthropomorphize the cosmological process through a religious lens.

This was the birth of the universe. It was done, the ultimate manifestation of energies: Creation. Light [Jesus] *was born out of the energy of consciousness and awareness of all that is. The star of the great central sun/Son was formed.*

But it did not stop there, for our Father [religious personification] *gathered this single point of existence, the Light of the singularity, His sun/Son from deep within the center of His stillness. He commanded, "Let there be Light!" With that, He hurled the Light across this new universe with His breath of life, prana, the energy of His life force.*

We see the first of many mentions of sun/Son, suggesting the words are interchangeable. The Bible frequently refers to Jesus (Son) as light (sun), calling Him the Light of the world, the Light of life, or a guiding Light.

These comparisons reveal the sun/Son link, thus connecting elements of religion with cosmology. Genesis 1:3 (KJM), "And God said, 'Let there be light: and there was light,'" proclaims both the arrival of His Son Jesus and the sun as the light of the singularity.

The nexus between science and religion continues:

> *An explosion of the Light of the singularity followed, an explosion of His awareness, an explosion of consciousness, extending beyond immeasurable boundaries. The singularity shattered and created an event horizon* [NASA: matter from an exploding star forms a singularity, resulting in a space-time boundary called an event horizon]. *As the center of this star exploded, it created a stargate.*

A stargate is a type of wormhole (Einstein-Rosen bridge) produced by excessive gravity from a black hole. Because of the theoretical nature of stargates, imagine my surprise when I find supporting information from NASA.

In an article published on August 17, 2022, NASA references "a gate of stars" in our galaxy which we pass through twice daily. Bringing this close to home, NASA writes, "The stargate is actually our Milky Way Galaxy, and it is the spin of the Earth that appears to propel you through it."

From the center of our Creator, energy exploded into spaces not previously known, for there had been no space before our Father commanded Light to come within.

And now, He had sent His sun/Son, His Light, across the ocean of nothingness into the infinite beyond, past the confines of the newly birthed universe, spreading both particles and waves [quantum physics] *of energy. Yet ever so faint, the heart of the singularity continued to beat.*

In Christian doctrine, the Trinity represents the unity of Father, Son, and Holy Spirit as three persons in one Godhead. The doctrine of the

The Word

Trinity is one of the central Christian affirmations about God.

In this message, we see the completion of the Holy Trinity. The Father had been born from consciousness/awareness of the Holy Spirit. Now the sun/Son, the Light of the world from the Bible, is born.

In an instant, the Light of the singularity washed over all that is. Many humans refer to this as the Big Bang.

I am amazed when my research corroborates these findings by none other than Albert Einstein. The message refers to the "Light of the singularity" as the Big Bang, just as Einstein's general theory of relativity references the "Big Bang Singularity" as the moment when all matter concentrates into a single point of infinite density (ScientificAmerican.com).

Energy from above crossed the soul of the singularity, extending below to anchor both dimensions through the energy of conscious awareness, creating the "as above, so below" concept. The horizontal explosion of the singularity produced an energy beam of consciousness that anchored the "as within, so without" dimensions.

The "as above, so below" and "as within, so without" concepts originate from the 2000-year-old sacred Hermetic text known as the Emerald Tablet of Hermes. These philosophies are part of the principles taught by Hermes Trismegistus, a "syncretic combination of the Greek god Hermes and the Egyptian god Thoth," (TheArchaeologist.org).

According to LearnReligions.com, these concepts suggest the idea of "the universe being composed of multiple realms (such as the physical and the spiritual) and that things that happen in one reflect upon the other."

I can't help but smile at the description. Isn't that precisely what the messengers did by showing me different interpretations of the same event, i.e., multiple realms reflecting upon the other?

At the intersection of the vertical and horizontal pillars, the soul of the singularity continued to beat, sending life-force energy to all that is. The Trinity [religious reference] *was complete, and the totality of its components shattered with the explosion of the singularity, spreading holographic particles of all that is to all there is, but its essence remained and continued to pulse.*

As I picture these words in my mind, I realize the intersecting pillars of vertical and horizontal energies form a cross. In the center of this religious representation lies a magnificent beating heart; it is the soul of the singularity, personifying both the sun and the Son.

The messengers blend cosmological and religious symbology. In doing so, they depict another great religious icon: the crucifixion.

Never before or since has there been such a massive eruption. The Creator hurled His own sun/Son from the center of His being into the new universe. As the energy from His sun/Son exploded within the newly formed universe, the multiverse formed.

Those exploding divine sparks from this great star created another dimension. The energy of the "as above, so below" and the "as within, so without" manifested as a great, multidimensional star, a merkaba, the great symbol of life from which all life sprang. It came to symbolize the energy and power behind all of creation.

When this enormous celestial object (representing the Son, Jesus) explodes, it becomes even greater; it transforms into the multidimensional star of a merkaba.

A merkaba is a star tetrahedron created by two intersecting pyramids, one pointing up and the other pointing down. This form is a significant part of sacred geometry because it embodies the foundational pattern for creation (SymbolsAndMeanings.net).

The star tetrahedron's two-dimensional version of two interlocking equilateral triangles creates a six-pointed star, a symbol associated with multiple cultures.

As the Star of David in Judaism, SymbolSage.com says three points of one star signify creation, revelation, and redemption; the remaining three tips represent man, the world, and God.

Mormon architecture uses the six-sided star to represent the union of heaven with our planet: humans reaching toward God while God reaches down toward us.

The message continues but with a twist, an unexplainable shift in perspective. I am no longer documenting the words entering my awareness; I begin speaking them.

> *And so it began. We were created from Light. Those pieces of the divine Light are the star seeds that were sown, for Light that was scattered from the beginning came from the great central sun/ Son, a great, magnificent star. We are those sparks of Light, shot forth from that sacred stargate. We are pieces of the singularity.*
>
> *But as the multiverse expanded, the Trinity* [religious reference to the three-sided pyramids of the merkaba] *began to separate until the point where we became lost. We strayed from the flock of the One Most Holy. We knew not from whence we came. We lost our homes, our sense of belonging, our true nature.*
>
> *We no longer knew our divinity within. We knew not that we came from Light. Like sheep that had wandered from the fold, we found ourselves lost in a wilderness, alone and afraid.*
>
> *The two pyramids of the star tetrahedron separated; one moved up as the other moved down. This created space and the perception of separation. This gap between the two pyramids became known to humanity as the veil. Humanity no longer felt*

connected to the Creator, our separation caused by the veil of forgetfulness.

As I speak these channeled words, I recognize the messenger's pattern of blending cosmic events with religious symbolism.

The singularity, in the shape of a star tetrahedron, explodes. As the merkaba splits, one three-sided pyramid disengages from the other, i.e., the trinity separates.

As this sacred star divides, we become its seeds. We are the star seeds cast into the universe/multiverse.

The parable of the lost sheep describes our dilemma: As we stray from "the flock of the One Most Holy," we become confused and isolated. At this point, as star seeds, we forget our sacred nature.

The separation of the Holy Trinity continued as the multiverse expanded, caused by the shattering of the great central sun/Son. The end result: many humans live their lives unaware of their connection to Source, to home, to Light, to the Creator.

Sacred geometry's symbol for creation, the

merkaba, is used to illustrate our separation from the Creator. As the two interlocking pyramids detach, a gap forms. No longer connected, the halves of the vehicle of light travel in opposite directions.

The chasm between the pyramids forms the "veil of forgetfulness," a barrier that prevents us from seeing our true nature, our true home. We star seeds not only disconnect from our sacred origins, but we also become oblivious.

But many are awakening to the truth that we are those flames cast off from the All-Mighty expression of energy. We are created from the magnificent Light source, the great star, the great sun/Son of the universe. It is a part of us, and we are a part of it, for we have come full circle.

There was a new Light, a new set of energy that was cast off from the great central sun/Son during creation. Yet this energy was different. It remained intact as a huge photon belt. This photon belt is now part of the ascension process for it is awakening the star seeds within each of us. The energy of the photon belt is similar to the energy of Source.

Could the photon belt's Source-like energy be responsible for my recent adrenaline rush? Had this energy fueled these extraordinary experiences?

A deep dive on the Internet reveals validations that leave me breathless. My research confirms the presence of a band of interdimensional light that travels across the Milky Way Galaxy every 26,000 years. Several Internet sites report Earth passes through this photon belt as part of a spiritual ascension (Quora.com).

I am surprised when the research verifies the presence of a cosmic band of light, but its role in our spiritual awakening astonishes me. This new light from the cosmic belt is the power behind humanity's ascension into higher realms.

A smile crosses my face when I connect the dots. Passing through this cosmic light jumpstarts our ascension, but the channeled words of the messengers indicate how. It is us, our star seeds.

As we awaken, we become enlightened. Our star seeds begin to shine, and these lights pierce the veil of forgetfulness, allowing us to step into full consciousness, pure awareness.

Changing my research focus to the central sun and a great central sun results in equally fascinating findings.

I am surprised at what I discover on EvenstarCreations.com. They report three suns align with a galactic center: our sun, the central sun, and the great central sun.

This celestial alignment produces significant spiritual shifts. As our Earth passes through the photon belt that originated from the central sun, Evenstar Creations concludes that people transform "to be the sun of our true self, the Son of God, Christed One."

The alignment of these three suns (three, referencing the Trinity) triggered the shift on December 21, 2012, that was previously discussed by the messengers, indicating energy-sensitive people would change. Evenstar Creations' website references a new sun that downloads additional light codes to prepare humanity to "step it up and become more at peace within and shine their light."

A new sun giving us different light? These thoughts brought me back to a set of messages and dreams that had informed me of changes in our sun. I had learned of cosmic entities who had given their sister star, our sun, a different set of energy frequencies to heal our planet.

Soon after receiving those older messages, in a vivid vision, I saw our Earth's great star morph into a lotus blossom with a thousand petals. Truly a flow-er of energy, this flower represents a perfect analogy for spiritual transformation caused by changes in our sun.

Chills dance up and down my spine when I consider these validations: the shift on December 21, 2012, the great central sun, the sun/Son connection, a photon belt, Earth's evolution, a new sun with different light, and humanity's move into a state of higher consciousness. I am speechless.

The Shepherd [Jesus, the Son] *is calling us home, back into the flock from which we came. As this new energy reaches us, entrainment occurs* [quantum physics].

Quantum physics teaches us that everything in the universe, from cells in our body to light and sound in the cosmos, is made of either particles or waves that communicate via vibrations. When two objects come in contact, often their frequencies become synchronous.

Once again, the messengers illustrate their

point through the lens of religious allegory. We witness entrainment as the flock returns to the Shepherd, and their frequencies become one with the sun/Son of the Creator.

The star seeds deep within our hearts are starting to vibrate to these new frequencies, taking on more Light, awakening from the deep slumber which has held us captive in a sea of forgetfulness. As our frequencies entrain to the newer energies, the ascension process awakens.

Our universe is no longer expanding but beginning to contract as we chart a course home to Source [cosmology: the Big Bang and the Big Bounce].

We are not separate from all that is. We are all one, for we have been birthed from the Light, and now it is time to return. It is time to know our Source, to recognize our Source, to love our Source, and to return to Source. It is time to awaken to our divinity within.

Look upon the sacred symbol of the merkaba and know ye are God. This is symbolic of creation, of return to the great central star/sun/Son within. It is symbolic of the New Order of Melchizedek which has come upon the Earth at this time to awaken the ascension process within.

Ye are born of the great central sun/Son. Allow that sacred star seed within to awaken.

My thoughts return to earlier messages involving the merkaba. A smile reaches my eyes when I contemplate its function. This structure is a vehicle of light, representing a balance between Earth and the cosmos, illuminating our paths to higher dimensions.

The merkaba is an ideal image to symbolize our connections to the sacred. This star tetrahedron heralds a New Earth.

Not only is this a sacred symbol of creation, but it also represents the New Order of Melchizedek. It's not the order where Jesus was a high priest, a lineage where the title passed through a specific ancestry.

This is a new order, representing current times, a birthright accessible to all. Through the New Order of Melchizedek, prepare yourself for a great awakening, one that, through a vehicle of light, will transport us to unseen realms of unity and love.

It all comes together, the images, the interpretations, this multidimensional approach connecting science with the spiritual.

I realize consciousness is a singularity that is merging with all beings, and it is ushering us into a New Earth.

> *Come dance with me. Dance with me in this Light that shines ever so brightly from within. Come dance with me through this beautiful new energy that has been given to us. Come dance with me, oh, ye children of the Light. Come dance with me in the Light.*

As these final words enter my awareness, an echo from the past causes my eyes to sparkle with tears. I recognize this lyrical language. It is from my first communication with the world of the nonphysical when unknown voices spoke to me about humans being flow-ers of energy.

A flash of remembrance reveals precisely when: August 28, 2013, a date permanently etched in my memory. Yes, The Muses Within are here to deliver the closing credits to the most profound experience of my life.

Other messengers from my past step forward. My cosmic friends from Alpha Centauri, Chiron, and the Pleiades are here, as are unnamed messengers who introduced valuable and stimulating concepts that enhance my life.

I feel the presence of angels and religious icons; I hold my breath in a failed attempt to staunch my tears when White Buffalo enters.

Surrounded by my beloved messengers, I drift into a dimension where neither time nor space exists. I've been here before, crossing many such thresholds over the past few years. Protected by my cosmic companions, I realize I am at the helm of my destiny. I smile, take a deep breath, and surrender.

As I acquiesce to the role of messenger, I realize I have returned to the opening scene: I am a flower of energy. Yet I never imagined this mystical launch into the unseen world of spirit would lead me to an even more significant beginning: creation.

Throughout my extraordinary journey, one question haunts me: Why me? Why had I been given opportunities to see beyond everyday reality into that mystical space outside of what the physical senses measure?

The answer had been validated; I had become an instrument, an agent for the messengers. I was to interpret and unveil these words to those ready to hear. Yet, I would share these lessons and ideas through *my* words.

My words. These are not the words of a prophet, an ascended master, or a saint but the words of a common, everyday person who has stepped on a path into the unknown. I may never know why the messengers chose me to be a representative, but I realize my acceptance of this challenge will transform me.

As I process these new responsibilities, the boundaries of my existence dissolve. A jumbled collection of fragmented moments from my life fade from view, and I know I can no longer pick up these threads of my old life. There's no going back.

I cannot stop the rush of tears when I realized this day will define me. How this would translate into my life is impossible to know. But one thing I can state with certainty: I will never be the same.

ACKNOWLEDGEMENTS

I would like to express my gratitude to those who helped make this book possible. I want to thank my family; I could not have written this book without your support. To my son, Phillip, who encouraged me to write from my heart. My daughter, Cassie, you inspire me with your endless energy as you balance all aspects of your life with grace. You lead by example, showing your girls the importance of family.

ACKNOWLEDGEMENTS

I want to recognize my much-loved granddaughters, Lorelai and Shalane. I've had such fun watching you grow. After all these years and life's twists and turns, I look over my shoulder as you girls play and see flashes with your mom as a child, moments forever etched in my memory. You both have enriched my life beyond measure.

Lorelai, you impress me with your unceasing desire to read. When you get quiet for five minutes, I know exactly where to find you: deeply engrossed in pages of a book. I'm equally amazed at your skills as an artist, a violinist, an Irish dancer, a budding chef extraordinaire, and an athlete. Your inner peace and serenity shine through your brilliant smile affecting everyone around you. Your innate kindness touches me deep within my soul.

Shalane, you are small but so mighty. Your fierce independence and infectious spirit make my heart sing, yet I melt in the wake of your magnetic smile. I'm fascinated by your endless desire to read about all living things from large cats and reptiles to all those creepy-crawly bugs. With your imaginative nature and your meticulous attention to detail, you create breathtaking pieces of art. You can do anything your beautiful heart desires. May you follow *White Buffalo's* whispered guidance with grace, ease, and conviction.

I want to thank my son-in-law, Dan, and my daughter-in-law, Kelly. You are the perfect spouses for Cassie and Phillip, and I could not love you more than if you had been my own.

I will always be grateful to Maryna Zhukova at MaryDes Designs for a book cover that magically captures the essence of the manuscript. Her interior book design and formatting skills are unsurpassed.

Finally, I thank those of you who have read my books, subscribed to my YouTube channels, or connected with me on social media. You make my journey worthwhile.

Did you like this book? If so, I'd love for you to show your gratitude by submitting a positive review on Amazon. Thank you!